W9-BMT-662

DISCARD

CATS

in the Zoo

CATS IN THE ZOO

BY ROLAND SMITH

Photographs by
WILLIAM MUÑOZ

THE NEW ZOO
THE MILLBROOK PRESS
BROOKFIELD, CT.

Library of Congress Cataloging-in-Publication Data

Smith, Roland, 1951—
Cats in the zoo / by Roland Smith
photographs by William Muñoz
p.   cm.—(The New zoo)
Includes bibliographical references (p.   ) and index.
Summary: Describes the habits of cats in the wild as
well as the care cats receive in today's zoo in order
to prevent their extinction.
ISBN 1-56294-319-7 (lib. bdg.)
1. Felidae—Juvenile literature.   2. Zoo animals—
Juvenile literature.   [1. Felidae.   2. Cats.
3. Zoo animals.]   I. Muñoz, William, ill.   II. Title.
III. Series: Smith, Roland, 1951—   New zoo.
QL737.C23S565   1994
599.74′428-dc20   93-1555   CIP   AC

Published by The Millbrook Press
2 Old New Milford Road
Brookfield, Connecticut 06804

Contents

The author and photographer wish to
thank the following organizations and
individuals for their help with this book:

Arizona-Sonora
Desert Museum

Cincinnati Zoo

Knoxville Zoo

Phoenix Zoo

Lincoln Park Zoo

Lowry Park Zoo
Point Defiance Zoo
and Aquarium

Reid Park Zoo

St. Louis Zoo

Bethany Kreilkamp

Jill Mellen

Marie Smith

Introduction

In the past, before we began to understand the harmful effects we were having on the earth and its wildlife, a zoo's main function was to entertain and amuse its human visitors. Today, many of the animals kept in zoos are not there just for our entertainment. They are there because it is no longer safe for them in the wild, and they are in danger of becoming extinct.

We could compare the new zoos to Noah's Ark— "lifeboats" for rescuing animals in danger of extinction. In this "ark" with the animals are their human keepers. During the voyage, the keepers do everything they can to make sure the animals survive and, if possible, reproduce in their artificial environment.

While the keepers are caring for the animals, they are also looking for "dry land"—wild habitat to which some of the animals might be returned. In the biblical story of Noah's Ark, after the flood, there were very few people on the earth and lots of wilderness areas. Today, there are many people and very few wilderness areas where animals can live in peace.

Wild cats are among the most majestic and powerful creatures in the animal kingdom and certainly one of the more popular animals in the zoo. Unfortunately, of the many species of cats in the world today, nearly all are either threatened or in serious danger of extinction.

This book is about wild cats—where they come from, what they are like, how they are cared for, and where their future lies. In many ways, their future depends on us.

The new zoo is a place for visitors to really experience cats—to watch a serval pounce on its prey, to hear a group of lions roar, to see a tigress play with her cubs. It is hoped that people who have seen what cats are like in the zoo will want to protect the future of cats in the wild.

This tiger shows four long, sharp teeth—its canines.

Cats
in the Wild

Near a watering hole in the wilds of India, a female tiger lies perfectly still in the dark night. She hears the rustle of dried leaves and slowly turns her head toward the sound. An axis deer cautiously steps out from the thick vegetation. The deer hesitates and tests the air for the scent of danger. The tigress watches but does not move. Sensing no danger, the deer walks to the edge of the water and lowers its head to browse on the tender shoots of grass growing along the shore. Silently, the tigress stands and gathers more information about her prey. The deer is 200 feet (60 meters) away from her—too far to rush in for the kill.

It has been more than a day since the tigress has eaten, but she knows from experience that to hurry is to go hungry. If she does not eat she will not be able to produce milk for her three cubs waiting a short distance away.

Ever so slowly she takes a step in the direction of the deer. As her giant paw touches the ground she freezes and watches and listens for any sign that her prey knows she is there. Step by step she closes the gap between herself and the deer.

The deer is faster than the tiger over a long distance. To succeed, the tigress must surprise the deer before it can flee.

When she is 30 feet (10 meters) away, she crouches in the long grass and does not take her eyes off the silhouette of the deer in the dim moonlight. The tip of her tail begins to flick from side to side.

The deer senses something. It stops eating and quickly lifts its head. It listens and smells the air, but it hears and smells nothing unusual because the tiger is downwind and silent. Satisfied that it is safe to start eating again, the deer lowers its head.

This is the moment the tigress has been waiting for. She tenses her powerful muscles and explodes from the grass. In less than three seconds she has covered the distance to her unsuspecting prey.

In one fluid movement, the tigress slams her 300-pound (135-kilogram) bulk into the deer and grasps its neck with razor-sharp claws. She pulls the deer to the ground and swiftly bites through its soft throat, crushing the windpipe. The tigress ignores the thrashing of sharp hooves and keeps the deer pinned to the ground. In a moment, the deer goes limp. The struggle is over.

The tigress holds on for a while longer as she catches her breath. Finally, she lets go and stands up. She grabs the deer by the neck and drags the body into the thick vegetation. Having found a secure spot, she slices off chunks of meat from the

A male Bengal tiger
from India.

A Bengal tiger on the
move. Its swiftness,
strength, and razor-
sharp teeth make a
deadly combination.

hindquarter with her scissorlike carnassial teeth and greedily gulps them down. For another day, her hunger is over.

Hunters • Teeth, claws, strength, speed, and stealth are the tools that cats use to hunt for food in the wild. They are so well equipped for hunting that they are sometimes called "perfect killing machines."

Cats have four long canine teeth that are used for grabbing and killing prey. Rows of carnassial teeth on the sides of the mouth work like scissors to slice meat and crunch bones. Incisors (front teeth between the canine teeth) are used for nibbling bits of meat off bones.

If you have ever been licked by a domestic cat you know that its tongue feels rough, like sandpaper. This is because the cat's tongue is covered with tiny spinelike structures that help it to scrape bones clean of meat.

Cats use their claws to catch and hold prey. To protect these sharp claws, they are able to pull them into special protective sheaths—much as we protect the sharpness of a hunting knife or a sword by putting the blade into a scabbard.

Cats come in a variety of different colors and patterns. The tiger has black vertical stripes against golden fur. These stripes offer camouflage, or a disguise, in the forest areas where they live. The spots on leopards, jaguars, and ocelots help conceal them in their bush and forest homes. Adult lions have tan-colored fur without spots or stripes. They blend in well with the grasses of the African savanna.

The hunt begins with a careful stalk and ends with an explosive rush of speed and power. Cats are very fast, but only over short distances. Even the cheetah, which can sprint more than 60 miles per hour (96 kilometers per hour), can keep up this speed for only a few minutes. Because of this, cats must get relatively close to their prey before making their final rush.

A cat may be designed to hunt and kill, but its prey is designed to get away. When this happens, the cat must start the whole hunting sequence over again.

What's more, being a hunter can be dangerous! Large cats such as lions and tigers can be seriously injured and sometimes killed by powerful kicks from their prey. Small cats can be bitten and scratched by the rodents they hunt.

Cats are generally more active during late evening and at night than during the day. One reason for this is that their prey is often out during these hours. Another reason that cats hunt at night is to avoid human contact.

Cats are well equipped to hunt at night. They can see approximately six times better than humans in the dark. Their eyes have a special mechanism in the retina called a *tapetum lucidum*, which reflects light back through the retina, doubling the intensity of dim light.

Cats are "opportunistic feeders," meaning they will hunt just about anything they can kill. The size of the prey depends on the size of the cat. Tigers and lions can kill large, hoofed animals such as deer and zebra, whereas small cats, such as ocelots and sand cats, kill rodents, birds, and lizards. Cats will also scavenge by feeding on the dead animals they find or by stealing food from other predators. They will also eat grasses, fruits, and berries, although this is a small portion of their diet.

Cats spend a great deal of time wandering through their territory—the specific area that they claim as their own—hunting for food and, during the breeding season, looking for a mate. When not hunting, they are usually resting. In fact, cats (domestic and wild) spend much of their lives either at rest or asleep.

Cubs • With the exception of lions and cheetahs, wild cats lead relatively solitary lives. Most female cats rear their youngsters without the help of a male.

The length of their pregnancy varies depending on the kind of cat. The tiny 2-pound (less than 1-kilogram) sand cat is pregnant for only 66 days before giving birth, whereas the 300-pound (136-kilogram) tiger is pregnant for as long as 103 days.

When a female is ready to give birth she finds a secluded spot where she will not be disturbed. She may use the abandoned burrow of another animal, a cave, a hollow tree, or even open ground protected by fallen trees or rocks.

The average litter size is one to four cubs (or kittens, as the young of small cats are called). The cubs are blind and helpless at birth. At two weeks their eyes open, and soon after this they start to explore the area near their den and to play with their litter mates.

Most of us have watched a domestic kitten play with a piece of yarn or a small ball. The kitten watches the object for several seconds or even minutes and then rushes in and attacks. Wild kittens and cubs play in the same way as domestic kittens. Instead of a piece of yarn or a ball they might play with a stick or a small rock. Young cats also stalk and wrestle with each other. This type of play helps to hone their hunting skills.

As the cubs get older they begin to venture farther from the den and to stalk small rodents and birds. At three to four months the cubs may begin to accompany their mother on her hunting trips. Cubs stay with their mother for six months to two years, depending on the species of cat.

Cat classification • Cats are sometimes called "felines" or "felids" because they belong to the family "Felidae" (fee-la-day), which is Latin for catlike.

Cats belong to the large order, or classification, called Carnivora, which includes meat-eating mammals that prey primarily on plant-eating animals. Dogs, bears, hyenas, otters, weasels, badgers, mongooses, and civets are also carnivores. One characteristic shared by all carnivores is that they have carnassial teeth for slicing meat. Other mammals, such as monkeys, apes, and humans, also eat meat, but they do not have slicing teeth and so are not considered carnivores.

Wild cats are found all over the world in a variety of habitats, from deserts to tropical rain forests. When we think of wild cats we usually think of large cats—lions, tigers, or leopards. But of the thirty-seven different species of cats, nearly half

The play of these puma cubs is a rehearsal for adulthood, when they will wrestle and bite to kill— and to survive.

are small, such as the 5-pound (2-kilogram) kodkod of Argentina and Chile, or the margay of Central and South America, which weighs between 6 and 9 pounds (2.7 and 4 kilograms).

Cats are classified as species, such as lions, tigers, and jaguars, and are further divided into subspecies. An animal may be classified as a subspecies because it is found in a different geographic area and has slightly different physical characteristics from others in the species. For instance, the tiger has eight subspecies, each living in a different part of the world, and each slightly different from the others in terms of size and coloration. The lion has two subspecies—one is found in Africa, the other in Asia.

Wild cats avoid human beings and so are seldom seen in their natural habitat. Much of what we know about their behavior and habits has been learned by studying them in zoos. This knowledge is used to help in the conservation of cats in the wild.

A Middle Eastern sand cat.

Exhibits
in the Zoo

In the last chapter we learned something about how cats function in the wild. Now we will look at how the wild is re-created in zoo exhibits.

Not many years ago, it was common to see cats in small, stark, iron-barred outdoor cages with concrete floors and in tile-covered indoor cages that looked like public rest rooms. These exhibits were easy to clean, but there was nothing for the cat to do in them except eat and sleep. Fortunately, most of these horrible cages have been torn down. In their place, zoos have built what are called naturalistic exhibits.

These exhibits try to duplicate a cat's natural environment. They have pools and streams for the cats to play in, grassy areas for them to lie on, bushes for them to hide behind, trees to climb, and logs on which they can sharpen their claws. To care for these naturalistic exhibits properly, keepers must know almost as much about plants as they do about their animals. But keepers feel that their cats are worth the extra effort.

Exhibit design • A "good" cat exhibit is large enough for the animal, escape-proof, safe for the cat and keeper, easy to manage the cat in, enjoyable to look at, simple to clean, and perhaps most important, a stimulating environment in which the cat can explore and display its natural behavior.

In some zoos, cat exhibits are grouped together in one area or building known as the "Cat House" or "Feline Building." In other zoos, they are spread throughout the zoo, usually grouped with other animals from a particular area of the world. A zoo may have an African area, for example, and in it will be many different animals from Africa, including lions and leopards. Another area may exhibit animals from South America and include jaguars and ocelots.

There are three basic barriers used to keep cats in their enclosures: moats, wire mesh, and glass.

A moat is a deep, wide ditch that runs along the front of an exhibit. It can be either dry or filled with water. Moats allow the zoo visitor to view the cats without any visual barrier. Generally only larger cats such as lions and tigers are kept in moated exhibits because they cannot jump or climb as well as some of the other cats. Cats that are good climbers and jumpers, such as leopards and pumas, are usually kept in exhibits with wire tops to prevent them from escaping.

The most common barrier used to contain cats is some type of wire. This might be welded wire, chain link, or piano wire.

Welded wire is probably the most common cat barrier. It comes in several sizes and is usually painted black, which makes it easier to see through.

Chain link, a surface of interwoven wires, is often used for large outdoor enclosures such as cheetah cages or off-exhibit breeding cages.

Piano wire is a thin wire that is stretched vertically on a frame to cover a viewing area. It is popular because it is almost invisible. But piano wire is only strong enough to serve as a barrier for smaller cats such as ocelots, clouded leopards, and snow leopards.

Glass is often used in indoor exhibits and outdoor viewing areas. One advantage glass has over wire is that it allows the visitor to experience the cat up close without risk of injury.

Cats aren't always on exhibit. Sometimes they are kept in holding areas, an important means of managing cats in captivity. They are places where cats are held while the keeper cleans the yard. Sick cats are isolated and treated in holding areas, and cats are often kept in them at night or during cold weather. These areas are also used to introduce cats to one another.

Their design is very simple. They are generally much smaller than the exhibit and out of public view. They usually have an elevated resting platform so the cat can be off the ground. In addition to this, holding areas have a slot, or "food-hopper," to put meat through, and a source of drinking water.

Ideally, each cat has its own holding area where it is trained to go at least once a day, usually during feeding time. While in the holding area, the keeper can get a good close look at each cat and make sure that it is in good health.

Environmental enrichment • To survive in the wild, cats must constantly make critical decisions relating to their environment. They have to find food, shelter, and water, defend their territories from competitors, and avoid human preda-

Glass barriers, like the one being cleaned in this photo, allow visitors to safely meet cats face-to-face.

This cat is being fed in a holding area. Attendants often isolate cats during meals to prevent fights over food and to make sure each cat gets enough to eat.

tors. In the zoo, cats do not have to make these kinds of decisions, because most of their needs are taken care of. To get cats to interact with their artificial environment, a few zoos are now experimenting with environmental enrichment programs. These programs are designed to relieve the problem of boredom by giving cats something to do besides eating and sleeping. Boredom can lead to stress, which causes physical and behavioral problems such as pulling out their fur (excessive self-grooming) and excessive pacing (stereotypic behavior).

Hiding food in the exhibit in difficult-to-reach places is a good environmental enrichment technique. The food might be hidden high up in the cage or inside a log or can. The cat has to figure out how to get to the food and, once there, how to get the food out of its hiding place. Another enrichment technique is to introduce live fish into the exhibit pool for the cats to catch.

Zoos do not often feed live prey to their cats. The cost is too high, and it is unfair to the prey. In the wild, a prey animal has a reasonable chance of escaping an attack by outmaneuvering or outrunning the cat. In an exhibit there is no place for the prey to get away.

A lion strolls with his trainer.

Cat
Husbandry

Animal husbandry is a complex process. Keepers must learn a lot about the animals under their care. They keep up with the latest research and rely on firsthand experience. In this chapter we will look at some of the specific techniques for helping cats survive, and prosper, in the zoo.

Animal husbandry begins the moment a wild cat arrives at the zoo. In the wild, most cats are solitary animals that only come together to breed. In the zoo, cats must learn to live with each other in relatively confined spaces. Even social cats, such as lions, need to be watched carefully. In the zoo, a lion that does not get along with a group has nowhere to go. In the wild, an outcast would be able to wander away and perhaps join another pride, or group, of lions. In the zoo this is not an option.

Getting cats together • Most zoos quarantine newly arrived cats before they are put in with the others. This is one way to prevent disease from being brought in from the outside. A quarantine period may last from thirty to sixty days, depending

This small quarantined leopard has
been anesthetized so that it can be
checked and treated by a veterinarian.

on the zoo's policy. During this time the new cat is examined and treated for any existing health problems. Before the new cat can mix with the others, it must be free of disease. When a cat has successfully completed quarantine it is transferred to the main zoo and introduced to its exhibit mate or mates.

Introducing new cats to each other can take anywhere from a few days to several months. To begin the introduction process the cats are kept in adjacent holding areas separated by a screen. The screen is used so they can interact without injuring each other. If the cats have not behaved too aggressively when separated by the screen, they are put into the same area for short periods of time. The amount of time the cats are in contact is gradually increased until finally they spend all of their time together.

Feeding cats • Years ago, zoos butchered meat to feed to their cats. They either raised livestock for this purpose, or they bought horses and cows from slaughterhouses. Today, most zoos use a commercial carnivore diet specially prepared to meet a cat's nutritional needs. This diet, which contains mostly horse meat, is often called a "feline diet." Zoos with large cat collections buy thousands of pounds of this meat every year and store it in large walk-in freezers. It comes in cases containing 5-pound (2-kilogram) packages of meat, making it easy for keepers to weigh out the right amount for each cat. Before being fed to the cats the meat is thoroughly thawed.

A jaguarudi, a small cat that lives in the southwestern U.S., among other places, enjoys a bowl of meat.

An attendant prepares to feed a beef bone to a tiger. The bone will help the cat's teeth to remain strong.

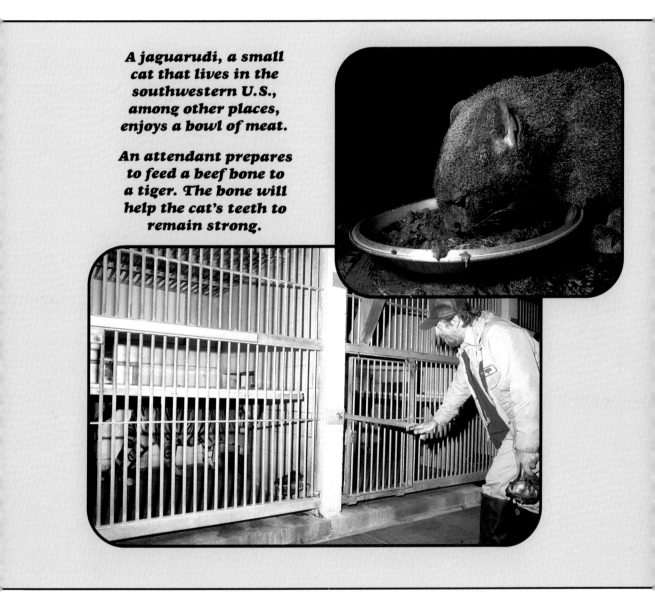

Cats are generally fed in their holding areas before the zoo opens for visitors. When possible, cats are fed separately to prevent fights from breaking out and to make sure that each cat gets the right amount of food. (If the cats have to be fed together, the keeper will usually stand and watch the group eat.) By feeding cats separately, keepers can track how much each cat is eating and write this down on the daily record. One of the first signs of illness in a cat is lack of appetite. If there is a drastic drop in the amount of food a cat eats, the cat may have to be examined by the zoo's veterinarian.

Because they are less active, cats in the zoo do not need as much food as wild cats. How much a cat is fed depends on the individual cat. One lion might be fed 10 pounds (4 kilograms) of meat a day, while another lion might be fed 8 pounds (3.5 kilograms) of meat a day. The amount depends on their weight and physical condition. Keepers try to keep their cats slim—a fat cat is an unhealthy cat.

In many zoos, cats are "fasted" one day a week, meaning that they are not fed on that day. The tradition of fasting zoo cats may come from the fact that, in the wild, cats often go without food for days at a time. However fasting started, it does not seem to hurt the cats; it helps to control their weight and it saves on the food bill.

Most zoos feed bones to their cats one or two days a week to help keep their teeth in shape. Large cats, such as lions and tigers, are fed large beef bones. Small cats, such as ocelots and servals, are fed chicken necks, dead mice, or dead rats.

Cleaning exhibits • Cleaning the cat exhibits is not the most glamorous part of a keeper's job, but it is extremely important. Cat exhibits, also called yards, are usually cleaned early in the morning while the cats are eating in their locked holding areas.

The procedure for cleaning an exhibit is pretty simple: Shovel up the stools; clean the pool if it needs it; hose the yard; take care of the plants; and wash the windows (if the enclosure is glass).

After the exhibit is cleaned, the keeper transfers the cat back into its yard. Holding areas are hosed and disinfected every day.

Escapes • Perhaps the keeper's biggest fear is to accidentally let a cat out, or for someone else to let a cat slip out while he or she is working in an exhibit.

Although attacks are rare, more than one keeper has been seriously mauled or killed by a cat that has escaped. Because of their size, big cats (lions, tigers, leopards, and jaguars) are the most dangerous. By nature, cats try to avoid people, and it is difficult to say what leads one to attack a keeper. The cat may think it is cornered and has no alternative but to lash out, or the cat may be surprised and, rather than run away, react aggressively. Regardless of its motivation, an unconfined cat is potentially very dangerous.

To lessen the risk of accidents, strict safety procedures are followed in each cat area. Cats are always locked in their holding areas when the keeper is cleaning the exhibit. In some zoos, signs are put on the holding areas warning others that there is a keeper in the yard and not to let the cat out. Other zoos use a "safety-lock" system. Safety locks are padlocks for which there is only one key. The keeper cleaning the exhibit locks the cat in the holding area with a safety-lock and carries the only key with him while he cleans the yard.

Each zoo has its own escape procedure. How an escape is handled depends on the circumstances of the escape and the kind of cat. The escape of a lion or tiger, for example, is handled differently from the escape of an ocelot.

If a cat gets loose inside a building, keepers try to prevent it from getting outside. Containing the cat in a relatively small area is the first step in capturing it. The keeper may use food to lure the cat back into its exhibit or holding area. If the cat is small, the keeper may be able to throw a net over it and carry it back to the exhibit. Obviously, using a net will not work on large cats, such as lions and tigers. To get them back where they belong a tranquilizer dart may have to be used.

A tranquilizer dart is fired from a special pistol, rifle, or blowgun. The dart itself is a syringe with a needle on the end of it. When the dart hits the cat, a tranquilizing drug is injected, and within about fifteen minutes the cat is sedated enough for the keepers to handle safely.

An escaped cat roaming the zoo grounds is very difficult to capture. Not only is the cat in an open area, but the keeper also has to worry about potential danger to zoo visitors. If the cat is in an isolated part of the zoo and no one is around, there may be time to try to entice it into a building or to shoot it with a tranquilizer dart.

If the cat is in a populated area, the zoo's first priority is to protect its visitors. Zoos have high-powered rifles for such emergencies and people trained to use them. Fortunately, however, these rifles are rarely used. The decision to shoot a cat is based on whether human life is in immediate danger. A cat is killed only as a last resort.

Handling cats • Although not a widespread practice, some zoos train a few of their cats. These cats are often used in educational talks for the public. Most trained cats in zoos were taken from their mothers at an early age and hand-reared. As a result, they are used to being handled by humans, which can make simple procedures, such as physical exams, easier.

From time to time other, untrained, cats must be caught to be examined or moved. How a cat is handled depends on what kind of cat it is. Nets and gloves may be used to catch small cats up to 15 pounds (7 kilograms). For cats over 15 pounds and under 40 pounds (18 kilograms) a snare, or catch-pole, is often used. A catch-pole is a hollow tube with a rubber-coated wire running through it and forming a noose at the tip. When the small cat is cornered, the keeper drops the loop over the cat's neck and shoulder and then tightens it by pulling on the wire at the tube's end.

A squeeze cage is a mechanical device used to restrain both

This tranquilizer dart
is shot from a dart gun.
Such darts are used to
subdue large cats in the
event of an escape.

This cheetah cub
had to be hand-reared
because its mother
neglected it.

small and large cats. It has one wall that can be moved inward to trap the animal so that it cannot move and injure itself while getting an injection. Most squeeze cages have a hand crank for moving the wall. As soon as the cat has gotten its injection, the wall is pulled back again. Some cats are made to pass through their squeeze cage every day on their way to their holding area. In this way they become used to the squeeze cage, which makes it easier to catch them when the need arises.

If a physical examination is going to take a long time or involves a painful procedure, the cat is tranquilized. Small cats are often manually restrained and given an injection with a hand-held syringe. For larger cats, other techniques are used, such as the tranquilizer dart or the "extension syringe," a long pole with a syringe on its tip. With this type of syringe the veterinarian can stand at a distance (outside the holding area) and inject the cat without handling it.

Baby cats • Captive breeding is one important way that zoos contribute to cat conservation. Very few cats come from the wild today—the majority of cats found in zoos were born there.

A couple of weeks prior to giving birth, a pregnant female cat is separated from the male and given access to a nest box, or a secluded holding area. To give the cat more security and privacy, the nesting area is often equipped with closed-circuit television so she can be observed without being disturbed.

The actual birth, and the forty-eight hours following birth, are critical times. During this period keepers watch the female twenty-four hours a day. They want to be certain that she does not have problems during the birth. If she does, they will call the veterinarian for assistance.

If the birth is normal, the next thing the keepers watch is the female's response to her cubs. Through inexperience or confusion cats have been known to neglect their own cubs or even to kill them. If it looks as if the female is going to harm her cubs or not feed them, the cubs may have to be taken and hand-reared in the zoo's nursery. Zoos are reluctant to take cubs from their mother because they know that hand-rearing is a poor substitute for a natural mother's care.

Whether the cubs are hand-reared or raised by their own mother, they are shipped to other zoos where they can contribute to cat conservation by producing cubs of their own.

4

A white tiger.

Different
Kinds of Cats

The wild cats of the world come in all sizes, from the tiny 2-pound (less than 1-kilogram) rusty-spotted cat of southern India to the magnificent 600-pound (270-kilogram) tiger of Asia. In this chapter we will look at some of the more common cats kept in zoos. We will learn how much they are fed, what type of exhibits they are kept in, how they rear their cubs, and what they are like in the wild.

Lion • The lion is often called the "king of beasts," which may come from the fact that adult males have dark, shaggy manes around their heads and shoulders that look something like crowns. No one knows for sure why the males have manes, but some biologists believe that they protect the male's head during fights with other males.

There are two types of lions, the African lion and the Asian lion. Of the two, the Asian is the rarest; only three hundred of them are left in the wild in India.

Male lions weigh from 330 to 550 pounds (150 to 250 kilograms). Females are considerably smaller, weighing between 265 and 400 pounds (120 to 180 kilograms). In the wild,

Although considered a small cat because it weighs in at no more than 45 pounds (20 kilograms), this African caracal is nevertheless fierce.

lions feed on a variety of large and medium-sized prey, including zebra, axis deer (spotted deer from India and Sri Lanka), and antelope. Lions are said to be able to consume as much as 77 pounds (35 kilograms) in one feeding, but on average a lion needs about 11 pounds (5 kilograms) of meat a day.

In the zoo, lions are fed between 8 and 12 pounds (3.6 to 5.5 kilograms) of meat a day and are fasted one day a week. Most zoos feed feline diet, but some zoos also feed carcasses to their lions, such as cows, calves, or road-killed deer. Lions are generally separated when fed to prevent fights from breaking out and to make sure that each cat gets its share of food.

Lions are "social" cats. In the wild they live in groups called prides. A pride can be made up of three to thirty individuals. A group of related lionesses and their cubs often form the core of the pride. The female cubs usually remain members of the pride. Male cubs are forced out when they are old enough to survive on their own. Some of them will eventually join another pride.

Living in a social group has many advantages. As a group, lions can hunt cooperatively and so increase their chances of killing prey and assure a more constant supply of food. In a pride the females are better able to protect their cubs, and should a female with cubs die, there is a chance that another female in the group will rear the dead female's cubs.

Zoos generally try to duplicate the pride structure by keeping a compatible group of lions together in a large open exhibit surrounded by a moat. Depending on the size of the exhibit, a

A lioness. Lion groups, or prides, exist for
the benefit of females. The lions band together
to protect the lionesses and their cubs.

captive lion pride can number anywhere between three and ten lions.

Females give birth to one to four cubs after a pregnancy of about 110 days. At birth, the cubs weigh a little over 3 pounds (a little over 1 kilogram) and are marked with spots that may stay on the legs and stomach until they are fully grown. The spots are thought to help camouflage the cubs when the female is off hunting.

In zoos, lionesses are often isolated in a holding area just prior to giving birth. As with other cats, male lions are generally separated from the female for several weeks afterward. As the cubs grow older they are sometimes slowly introduced to the male through an introduction screen. After a period of time, if the male does not become aggressive, keepers will open the screen and allow him to join the female and cubs.

In the wild, cubs stay with their mothers for up to two years. Zoos try to keep cubs with the pride as long as possible.

Tiger · The lion may be considered the king of beasts, but the tiger is a bigger cat. The male Bengal tiger from India weighs between 440 and 595 pounds (200 and 270 kilograms), and females weigh from 275 to 355 pounds (125 to 160 kilograms). A male Siberian tiger can weigh as much as 700 pounds (317 kilograms).

The rarest tiger in the world is the South China tiger. Fewer than fifty of them remain in the wild, and only two hundred are found in zoos. Some zoos keep white tigers, which are very popular with zoo visitors. The white tiger is not a true subspecies but a mutated form of the common Bengal or Siberian tiger.

Tigers are found in India, Pakistan, Nepal, Bhutan, Bangladesh, Thailand, Vietnam, the Commonwealth of Independent States, and parts of China. In the wild they can live in a variety of habitats, but they require sufficient cover, year-round access to water, and, of course, a steady supply of large prey animals. They eat wild pig, cattle (domestic and wild), and several species of deer. They are capable of gorging on meat, consuming as much as 60 to 80 pounds (27 to 36 kilograms) in one night.

In the wild, female tigers spend a good portion of their lives accompanied by successive litters of dependent young. Male tigers live alone for the most part, although it has been reported that adults will come together to share a kill.

In zoos, tigers are fed up to 8 pounds (3.5 kilograms) of feline diet a day. To avoid fighting they are usually fed separately in their holding areas. Like most cats they are fasted one day a week and are periodically fed large beef bones.

Tigers are kept in pairs or small groups in large moated exhibits. Exhibits usually have pools because tigers enjoy swimming and soaking, especially when it is hot outside.

Females give birth to two to four young after a pregnancy of about 103 days. To protect the cubs from harm, males are generally separated from the female during the time that she raises the young. In the wild, cubs stay with their mother for eighteen to twenty months. In the zoo, cubs are usually kept with their mother until she has another litter.

Jaguar • Not as well known as the lion and tiger, the jaguar is the third-largest cat in the world. It weighs up to 300 pounds (135 kilograms), although, on average, male jaguars weigh 120 pounds (55 kilograms) and females weigh around 80 pounds (36 kilograms).

Jaguars are found in south central Mexico, Central America, and parts of South America. They are powerfully built with a large broad head and short sturdy limbs. With their spotted fur they look a lot like a stocky leopard; however, the rings, or rosettes, on leopards and jaguars differ. The jaguar has rosettes with one or two spots in the middle; the leopard's rosettes have no spots in the middle.

Jaguars come in two color phases—the spotted and the black. Black jaguars are not a separate species of jaguar; they are simply a different color phase called "melanistic," meaning black. If the light is just right, you can see that the black jaguar has spots, too.

In the wild, jaguars are usually found near streams, rivers, and lakes. They will feed on almost anything they can find—lizards, snakes, caiman (crocodiles), fish, turtles, small mammals, deer, and domestic cattle.

Jaguars are solitary in the wild, but in zoos they are kept in pairs. They are generally fed separately and given an average of 5 pounds (2 kilograms) of feline diet a day.

They are excellent climbers, so in zoo exhibits they are provided with sturdy branches to climb and platforms to lie on. Like tigers, jaguars enjoy the water, and they are provided with pools where they can soak and swim.

Jaguars give birth to between two and four young after a pregnancy of about 100 days. The young weigh a little under 2 pounds (1 kilogram) when they are born. Like most cats, the female jaguar has the sole responsibility for rearing the cubs. Young jaguars stay with their mother for up to two years.

In the zoo, the female is separated from the male while she raises her cubs. The cubs are weaned at six to twelve months, and they usually stay with their mother until she has another litter.

No one knows how many jaguars remain in the wild, but it is estimated that only a thousand are left in Mexico and Central America. The decline of the jaguar is directly linked to the destruction of the tropical rain forest.

Cheetah • The cheetah, the fastest land mammal on earth, weighs between 80 and 150 pounds (36 and 68 kilograms), and lives in the open plains of southern, central, and eastern Africa and in the Middle East, where it is almost extinct. The cheetah preys on medium-sized hoofed animals, such as gazelles and impalas. To catch these swift animals, the cheetah stalks to within about 30 feet (10 meters) of them and then explodes with a burst of speed. The cheetah's sprint lasts less than a minute, and chases result in kills only about half of the time.

**Long-legged and lightning-fast, the cheetah
has been clocked at speeds of close
to 70 miles (110 kilometers) per hour.**

Female cheetahs live alone, except when they are rearing cubs. Males live alone or in male groups of two to four, called coalitions.

In zoos, cheetahs are kept in compatible groups in large open exhibits where they can run and exercise. These exhibits are often nothing more than large fenced compounds with wire holding areas and a shelter. Zoos feed their cheetahs about 2.5 pounds (1.1 kilograms) of feline diet, chicken, and rabbit each day.

After a pregnancy of ninety to ninety-five days, females give birth to an average of three to five cubs (but as many as eight). At birth the cubs weigh less than a pound, and they will stay close to their mother until they are over a year old. Zoos leave the cubs with their mothers for as long as possible before shipping them to other zoos.

Leopard • The leopard looks like a slender jaguar. Males weigh between 80 and 100 pounds (36 and 45 kilograms); females weigh between 60 and 75 pounds (27 and 34 kilograms). The black color phase is common.

Leopards live throughout many countries in the Eastern Hemisphere. They are found throughout Africa (except the Sahara), in the Middle East, throughout Pakistan and India, and in Southeast Asia, China, and Siberia. Despite this wide distribution, several subspecies of leopard are highly endangered.

Leopards are very adaptable cats; they can survive almost

anyplace where there is enough food and shelter. They are known to live near the suburbs of Nairobi, Kenya, and other African cities, where they kill dogs and cats for food (much as coyotes live near the suburbs of Los Angeles, and foxes and raccoons live in the middle of Washington, D.C.).

In the wild, leopards will eat just about anything from insects to rodents to larger prey such as gazelle, deer, pig, and monkey. To stop lions, tigers, and hyenas from taking their food, leopards will store their kills in the branches of trees.

In the zoo, leopards are fed 2 or 3 pounds (about 1 to 1.3 kilograms) of feline diet a day and are sometimes also fed chickens, rabbits, and rodents. They are occasionally fed bones and are generally fasted one day a week. To avoid fights over food they are separated when they are fed.

Females give birth to two or three young after a pregnancy of 90 to 105 days. The cubs weigh about a pound (0.45 kilogram) at birth and in the wild stay with their mother for a year and a half to two years. As with other cats, zoos keep the cubs with their mother for as long as they can.

Puma · The puma is the largest of the wild cats found in the Americas. It is also known as a mountain lion, American lion, cougar, and panther. The puma is found throughout Canada and the United States (west of the Great Plains) and in southern Florida, Mexico, Central America, and South America. It is about the size of a leopard, although its weight varies depending on where it is found. Males weigh between 150 and 170

A puma peers out from tall grass.

pounds (68 and 77 kilograms); females weigh much less—between 90 and 100 pounds (40 and 45 kilograms). Like the lion, the puma is plain-colored, but the cubs are born with spots that help to camouflage them when they are young.

In the wild, pumas eat elk, deer, beaver, porcupine, rabbit, raccoon, opossum, and wild hog. In zoos they are fed about 2.5 pounds (about 1 kilogram) of feline diet a day, and their diet is periodically supplemented with whole rabbits and chickens as well as with bones to keep tartar from building up on their teeth.

Females give birth to three or four cubs after a pregnancy of 90 to 95 days. Young pumas stay with their mother until they are about two years old, and they may then travel with each other for a few months after leaving her.

Snow Leopard • The snow leopard is one of the rarest and most beautiful cats. It weighs between 55 and 165 pounds (24 and 75 kilograms) and has gray-green eyes and long cream-colored fur with black spots. The snow leopard's tail is thick and almost as long as its body. The tail helps the cat balance as it moves across rocky terrain. Some people claim that the snow leopard wraps its tail like a muffler across its nose and face to keep warm in the icy wind.

These exotic leopards are found in the mountainous regions of central Asia and in the former Soviet Union, Mongolia, China, Nepal, Bhutan, India, Pakistan, and possibly Afghanistan.

Although so rare they were once thought to be mythical, snow leopards, like the one shown here, can be seen in many zoos today.

In the wild, snow leopards prey on wild sheep and goats, marmots, musk deer, rabbits, and birds. In zoos they are fed about 5 pounds (2.3 kilograms) of feline diet a day in addition to periodic feedings of rabbits and chickens.

Not much is known about the snow leopard's social behavior, but adult pairs have been seen traveling and hunting together in the wild.

In the zoo, snow leopards are kept in pairs. Females give birth to two or three cubs after a pregnancy of 90 to 103 days. The male and female are separated when the female has young.

Serval · The serval is a spotted cat with long legs, big ears, and a short tail. It is a small-sized cat, weighing between 20 and 40 pounds (9 and 18 kilograms), and is found in the open grasslands of Africa, usually near water.

Servals use their sensitive hearing to locate rodents moving in the tall grass. Once its prey is pinpointed, the serval sneaks up to within a few feet of the rodent and pounces. Aside from rodents, servals eat small birds, frogs, lizards, and insects.

In zoos they are fed about one-half pound (0.2 kilogram) of feline diet a day. Periodically, keepers will also feed them chicken parts, rats, and mice.

Servals are kept in pairs, but are separated when the female has young. Females give birth to one to three kittens after a pregnancy of about 74 days.

Like the jaguar and the leopard, "black" servals have been reported, although these are relatively rare.

A group of newborn servals.

Ocelot · Ocelots are beautiful spotted cats found in southern Texas, parts of Mexico, Central America, and in South America east of the Andes to northern Argentina. Males weigh between 20 and 30 pounds (9 and 13 kilograms). Females weigh between 15 and 25 pounds (7 and 11 kilograms).

Ocelots are thought to hunt mostly at night by stalking a variety of prey—small mammals, birds, fish, snakes, and lizards.

In the zoo they are fed approximately a half-pound (0.2 kilogram) of feline diet a day and periodically supplemented with whole rodents and chicken parts.

Although not much is known about the social behavior of ocelots in the wild, it is assumed that they are solitary. In the zoo they are kept in pairs until the female gives birth.

Females have two to four kittens after a pregnancy of 79 to 82 days. Like the serval (and most other small cats), prior to birth they are provided with den boxes to have their kittens in. These boxes are often equipped with video cameras so that keepers can keep an eye on the development of the kittens.

A puma cub.

Cat
Conservation

Almost all of the wild cats found in the world are threatened with extinction in some way. Nearly half of the thirty-seven species of cats are classified as endangered, which means that an animal is on the verge of extinction.

Why cats are in trouble • One reason that so many cats have been killed is the fur trade. Some people think that the spotted skin of a cat looks better on them than it does on a living cat. Tens of thousands of cats have been killed in the name of "fashion." In the early 1970s the United States imported 25,000 large-cat skins (leopards, tigers, and jaguars) and over 130,000 ocelot skins a year. In 1980, Europe imported nearly a half million cat skins in all.

Fortunately, the Endangered Species Act, which was passed in 1973, makes it illegal to import spotted cat fur into the United States. Unfortunately, this ban caused a problem for two cats native to the United States—the bobcat and the lynx—because they have spotted fur. The value of their fur increased from $15 a pelt to as high as $225 a pelt.

Another practice affecting the number of cats in the wild is trophy hunting. The lion, jaguar, leopard, and even the highly endangered snow leopard are still hunted legally in some countries. In the United States it is legal to hunt the bobcat and puma in many states.

The biggest factors contributing to the cat's extinction are habitat destruction and the construction of roads in wilderness areas. The new roads allow poachers and hunters access to previously untouched cat populations. As our human population increases we use more land, which means less land is left for cats and other wild animals.

Without enough habitat in which to hunt, cats either starve or are forced to prey on domestic livestock. This causes conflicts between cats and humans. To protect their livelihood, ranchers trap, poison, and shoot cats.

Cat conservation in the zoo · Zoos from all over the world work together to save animals from extinction. Zoos no longer consider themselves the "owners" of the animals they house but their "custodians." As custodians, their responsibility is to manage each animal in such a way that the entire species benefits.

Many animals in zoos are managed under a program called the Species Survival Plan. Animals managed under this plan are treated as a single group rather than individually by each zoo. Thus, management decisions can be made that will benefit the whole species (wild and captive) rather than just one animal.

One of the main tools of the Species Survival Plan is the studbook. Each animal in the program is assigned a studbook number. By looking up the animal's number, a keeper can learn whether the animal was captured in the wild or born in captivity, who its parents are, its date of birth, and its current location. With this information keepers can decide which animals should be bred to improve the overall captive population.

Currently there are Species Survival Plans for tigers, snow leopards, clouded leopards, cheetahs, and Asian lions. There will soon be studbooks for every wild cat species in the world.

A new emphasis is being placed on breeding programs for the smaller wild cats. Zoos have come to realize that they have ignored these little felines in favor of the bigger, more popular cats. As a result, there are very few small cats in zoos, and little is known about how many of them still live in the wild.

Aside from the Species Survival Plan, zoos are helping wild cats in many other ways.

Much of what we know about cat biology (such as breeding biology) has been learned in zoos. By continuing to learn about cats in zoos, biologists are able to help cats in the wild.

In some parts of the world, cats are killed because of conflicts with the expanding human population. Zoos provide an alternative to killing them by making space available for these cats in their collections.

Another way that our zoos help cats in the wild is to share their expertise. Zoo workers travel to other countries to instruct people in the care and breeding of cats in captivity. With this knowledge, these countries can also set up captive breeding programs for their own endangered cats. If zoos build up a big enough captive cat population they will one day have sufficient animals to release back into the wild should this be necessary and possible.

Aside from providing a sanctuary for many of the world's cats, zoos give visitors an opportunity to see these magnificent creatures up close and learn something about them. With this knowledge people have a better understanding of the plight of the cat in the wild.

How you can help save cats • Nearly half of the cat species are found in the world's tropical rain forests. In the last decade we have lost nearly 20 percent of these irreplaceable habitats. No one knows for sure how many cats have died as a result of this loss.

One way to help the cats of the world is to protect the habitats in which they live. This can be done by creating wildlife preserves and parks in which it is illegal to trap and kill animals. You can help protect land by joining and supporting organizations whose primary goal is to preserve the world's dwindling habitats.

You and your friends and classmates can write letters to local politicians, telling them of your concerns and asking them what they are doing to solve the problem of dwindling habitats. You can also write to the leaders of tropical nations and ask them what they are doing to protect their natural habitats.

Another thing you can do is support your local zoo and its programs to preserve animals. The average zoo takes up less than 55 acres (22 hectares). If we were to put all the zoos together, there would be less then 31 square miles (80 square kilometers) of captive habitat. A zoo cannot produce more animals than it can hold. Many zoos are trying to increase the amount of space they have for endangered animals by buying large tracts of land to be used as captive breeding facilities. You can help by volunteering your time and helping zoos raise money for wildlife conservation.

In a way you have already helped a little to save cats from extinction by reading this book. But understanding the problem is only part of the solution. You need to share what you have learned with your family, friends, and classmates. The more people who are aware of a problem, the better chance there is of solving it.

You may think that the problems of extinction and habitat loss belong to someone else or that someone else will take care of them. But these problems are shared by all of us who live on the earth.

Glossary

Carnassial teeth. Special teeth, used to slice meat, found in carnivores.

Conservation. The controlled use and protection of natural resources.

Endangered species. An animal that does not have enough of its kind left to maintain or increase its population.

Extinction. What happens when the last animal of a species dies.

Habitat. An area or environment where a biological organism lives.

Husbandry. The breeding, raising, and care of animals.

Nocturnal animal. An animal that sleeps during the day and is active at night.

Pregnancy. The period of time that a female carries her offspring before birth.

Quarantine. A period of time that an animal is kept apart from other animals to make sure that it is not carrying a contagious disease.

Social order. The ranking order of any social animal group. An animal's rank in the order is determined by strength, age, leadership abilities, intelligence, sex, and other factors.

Species. A category of classification for different organisms. Animals within a species are grouped together because of their similarities.

Species Survival Plan. A conservation plan whereby animal species, such as tigers, are managed as a single group, regardless of which zoo is keeping them.

Studbook. A species record that tells who an individual animal's parents are, its date of birth, and its sex. The studbook is used by zoologists to pick animal pairs for breeding.

Subspecies. A subdivision of animal classification, often based on geographical location. (See: Species)

Further Reading

Caras, Roger. *A Cat Is Watching*. New York: Simon and Schuster, 1989.

Caras, Roger. *Mara Simba: The African Lion*. New York: Holt, Rinehart and Winston, 1985.

Guggisberg, C.A.W. *Wild Cats of the World*. New York: Taplinger Publishing Company, 1975.

Hillard, Darla. *Vanishing Tracks*. New York: Arbor House/William Morrow, 1989.

Jackson, Peter. *Endangered Species: Tigers*. New York: Chartwell Books Inc., 1990.

Kitchener, Andrew. *The Natural History of the Wild Cats*. Sausalito, Cal.: Comstock Publishing Editions, 1991.

Leyhausen, Paul. *Cat Behavior: The Predatory and Social Behavior of Domestic and Wild Cats*. New York: Garland Press, 1979.

McMullen, James P. *Cry of the Panther: Quest of a Species*. New York: McGraw Hill Book Company, 1984.

Morris, Desmond. *Cat Watching*. New York: Crown Publishers Inc., 1986.

Rabinowitz, Alan. *Chasing the Dragon's Tail: The Struggle to Save Thailand's Wild Cats*. New York: Doubleday, 1991.

Ryden, Hope. *Bobcat Year*. New York: Viking Press, 1981.

Sankhala, Kailash. *Tiger! The Story of the Tiger*. New York: Atheneum, 1965.

Schaller, George B. *The Serengeti Lion: A Study of Predator-Prey Relations*. Chicago: University of Chicago Press, 1972.

Seidensticker, John, & Lumpkin, Susan (editors). *Great Cats: Majestic Creatures of the Wild*. Emmaus, Pa.: Rodale Press, 1991.

Whitfield, Philip. *The Hunters*. New York: Simon and Schuster, 1978.

Index